WILDLIFE SANCTUARIES

Delaware Ecoregions

- ☐ Middle Atlantic Coastal Plain
- ■ Southeastern Plains
- ☐ Northern Piedmont

1. Ashland Nature Center
2. Brandywine Creek State Park
3. Lums Pond State Park
4. Pea Patch Island
5. Cedar Swamp Wildlife Area
6. Blackiston Wildlife Area
7. Bombay Hook National Wildlife Refuge (NWR)
8. Little Creek Wildlife Area
9. Norman G. Wilder Wildlife Area
10. Killens Pond State Park
11. Abbott's Mill Nature Center
12. DuPont Nature Center
13. Prime Hook NWR
14. Beach Plum Island Nature Preserve
15. Cape Henlopen State Park
16. Barnes Woods Nature Preserve
17. Delaware Seashore State Park
18. Nanticoke Wildlife Area
19. Trap Pond State Park
20. Great Cypress Swamp
21. Assawoman Wildlife Area

DELAWARE WILDLIFE

A Folding Pocket Guide to Familiar Animals

DELAWARE WILDLIFE – A Folding Pocket Guide to Familiar Animals

WATERFORD PRESS

SEASHORE LIFE

Sea Nettle
Chrysaora quinquecirrha
To 10 in. (25 cm)

Common Sea Star
Asterias forbesi
To 10 in. (13 cm)
May be tan, brown, orange or olive with orange highlights.

Moon Jellyfish
Aurelia aurita
To 16 in. (40 cm)
Commonly washed up on beaches after storms.

Common Slipper Snail
Crepidula fornicata
To 2 in. (5 cm)

Northern Moon Snail
Lunatia heros
To 4.5 in. (11 cm)

Atlantic Bay Scallop
Argopecten irradians
To 3 in. (8 cm)

Northern Quahog
Mercenaria mercenaria
To 5 in. (13 cm)
Found in mud near low tide mark.

Eastern Oyster
Crassostrea virginica
To 10 in. (25 cm)

Sand Dollar
Echinarachnius parma
To 3 in. (8 cm)
Skeletons, called 'tests,' often wash up on beaches.

Lady Crab
Ovalipes ocellatus
To 2 in. (5 cm)
Aggressive crab has sharp pincers.

Knobbed Whelk
Busycon carica
To 9 in. (23 cm)
Note prominent knobs on spire.

Blue Mussel
Mytilus edulis
To 4 in. (10 cm)
Grows attached to pilings and other marine objects.

Fiddler Crab
Uca spp.
To 1.5 in. (4 cm)

Blue Crab
Callinectes sapidus
To 9 in. (23 cm)

Horseshoe Crab
Limulus polyphemus
To 12 in. (30 cm) wide.
Delaware's state marine animal.

Northern Rock Barnacle
Balanus balanoides
To 1 in. (2.5 cm)

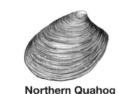
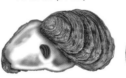

INSECTS & SPIDERS

Ladybug Beetle
Family Coccinellidae
To .5 in. (1.3 cm)
Red wing covers are black-spotted.
Delaware's state insect.

Black-and-yellow Garden Spider
Argiope aurantia
To 1.25 in. (3.2 cm)

Green Darner
Anax junius
To 3 in. (8 cm)
Like most dragonflies, it rests with its wings open.

Ebony Jewelwing
Calopteryx maculata
To 1.75 in. (4.5 cm)
Like most damselflies, it rests with its wings held together over its back.

Northern Bluet
Enallagma annexum
To 1.5 in. (4 cm)

Stonefly
Order Plecoptera
To 2.5 in. (6 cm)
Delaware's state macroinvertebrate.

Eastern Tiger Swallowtail
Papilio glaucus
To 6 in. (15 cm)
Delaware's state butterfly.

Red-spotted Purple
Limenitis arthemis astyanax
To 3.5 in. (9 cm)

Red Admiral
Vanessa atalanta
To 2.5 in. (6 cm)

Mourning Cloak
Nymphalis antiopa
To 3.5 in. (9 cm)
Emerges during the first spring thaw.

Viceroy
Limenitis archippus
To 3 in. (8 cm)
Told from similar monarch by its smaller size and the thin, black band on its hindwings.

Monarch
Danaus plexippus
To 4 in. (10 cm)

Baltimore Checkerspot
Euphydryas phaeton
To 2.5 in. (6 cm)

Luna Moth
Actias luna
To 4.5 in. (11 cm)

Little Virgin Moth
Grammia virguncula
To 2 in. (5 cm)

Cecropia Silkmoth
Hyalophora cecropia
To 6 in. (15 cm)

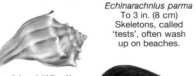

FISHES

Weakfish
Cynoscion regalis   To 3 ft. (90 cm)
Back is covered with small spots.
Delaware's state fish.

Largemouth Bass
Micropterus salmoides   To 40 in. (1 m)
Note prominent stripe down side, jaw extends past eye.

Bluefish
Pomatomus saltatrix   To 43 in. (1.1 m)
Short first dorsal fin has 7-8 spines.

Smallmouth Bass
Micropterus dolomieu   To 27 in. (68 cm)
Jaw joint is beneath the eye.

American Shad
Alosa sapidissima   To 30 in. (75 cm)
Note line of spots behind gill cover.

Crappie
Pomoxis spp.   To 16 in. (40 cm)

Bluegill
Lepomis macrochirus   To 16 in. (40 cm)

Pumpkinseed
Lepomis gibbosus   To 16 in. (40 cm)

Yellow Perch
Perca flavescens   To 16 in. (40 cm)
Note 6-9 dark 'saddles' down its side.

Rainbow Trout
Oncorhynchus mykiss   To 44 in. (1.1 m)

Black Drum
Pogonias cromis   To 6 ft. (1.8 m)

Striped Bass
Morone saxatilis   To 6 ft. (1.8 m)
Has 6-9 dark side stripes.

Spanish Mackerel
Scomberomorus maculatus   To 3 ft. (90 cm)

Flounder
Paralichthys spp.   To 3 ft. (90 cm)

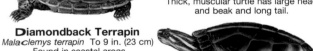

REPTILES & AMPHIBIANS

Spring Peeper
Pseudacris crucifer   To 1.5 in. (4 cm)
Note dark X on back. Musical call is a series of short peeps.

Green Treefrog
Hyla cinerea   To 2.5 in. (6 cm)
Call is a cowbell-like – clank.

Bullfrog
Lithobates catesbeianus   To 8 in. (20 cm)
Call is a deep-pitched – jug-o-rum.

Tiger Salamander
Ambystoma tigrinum   To 13 in. (33 cm)
Pattern of yellowish and dark blotches is variable.

Red-backed Salamander
Plethodon cinereus   To 5 in. (13 cm)

Snapping Turtle
Chelydra serpentina   To 20 in. (50 cm)
Thick, muscular turtle has large head and beak and long tail.

Diamondback Terrapin
Malaclemys terrapin   To 9 in. (23 cm)
Found in coastal areas.

Painted Turtle
Chrysemys picta picta   To 10 in. (25 cm)
Note red marks on outer edge of shell.

Broad-headed Skink
Plestiodon laticeps   To 13 in. (33 cm)
Woodland skink is often seen in trees.

Common Garter Snake
Thamnophis sirtalis sirtalis
To 4 ft. (1.2 m)
Black, brown or greenish snake has three yellowish stripes.

Northern Water Snake
Nerodia sipedon   To 4.5 ft. (1.4 m)
Note dark blotches on back.

Black Rat Snake
Elaphe obsoleta   To 8 ft. (2.4 m)
Chin and throat are white or cream.

Northern Black Racer
Coluber constrictor
To 6 ft. (1.8 m)

Copperhead
Agkistrodon contortrix   To 52 in. (1.3 m)
Venomous snake has hourglass-shaped bands down its back.

Eastern Kingsnake
Lampropeltis getulus getulus
To 7 ft. (2.1 m)
Brown to black snake has a light, chain-like pattern down its back.

Timber Rattlesnake
Crotalus horridus   To 6 ft. (1.8 m)
Has a black tail. Venomous.

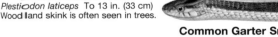

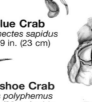

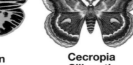

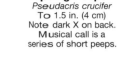
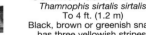
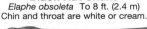

Snow Goose
Chen caerulescens
To 31 in. (78 cm)
Up to 200,000 winter at
Bombay Hook NWR.

Canada Goose
Branta canadensis
To 45 in. (1.14 m)

Double-crested Cormorant
Phalacrocorax auritus
To 3 ft. (90 cm)
Note orange-yellow
throat patch.

Mallard
Anas platyrhynchos
To 28 in. (70 cm)

Northern Pintail
Anas acuta To 30 in. (75 cm)

Wood Duck
Aix sponsa To 20 in. (50 cm)

Common Loon
Gavia immer To 3 ft. (90 cm)

Winter

Summer

Great Egret
Ardea alba
To 38 in. (95 cm)
Note yellow bill
and black feet.

American Oystercatcher
Haematopus palliatus
To 20 in. (50 cm)

Glossy Ibis
Plegadis falcinellus
To 26 in. (65 cm)

Great Blue Heron
Ardea herodias
To 4.5 ft. (1.4 m)

Black-crowned Night-Heron
Nycticorax nycticorax
To 28 in. (70 cm)

Ring-billed Gull
Larus delawarensis
To 20 in. (50 cm)
Bill has dark ring.

Great Black-backed Gull
Larus marinus
To 32 in. (80 cm)
Told by large size
and dark back.

Delaware Blue Hen
To 5 lbs. (2.2 kg)
Non-native cock-fighting
chicken is the **State
Bird of Delaware.**

Northern Bobwhite
Colinus virginianus
To 12 in. (30 cm)

Rock Pigeon
Columba livia
To 13 in. (33 cm)

Mourning Dove
Zenaida macroura
To 13 in. (33 cm)
Call is a mournful –
ooah-woo-woo-woo.

Wild Turkey
Meleagris gallopavo
To 4 ft. (1.2 m)

Ruby-throated Hummingbird
Archilochus colubris
To 3.5 in. (9 cm)

Downy Woodpecker
Picoides pubescens
To 6 in. (15 cm)
The similar hairy
woodpecker is larger
and has a longer bill.

Northern Flicker
Colaptes auratus
To 13 in. (33 cm)
Wing and tail
linings are yellow.

Belted Kingfisher
Megaceryle alcyon
To 14 in. (35 cm)

Bald Eagle
Haliaeetus leucocephalus
To 40 in. (1 m)

Osprey
Pandion haliaetus
To 2 ft. (60 cm)

Red-tailed Hawk
Buteo jamaicensis
To 25 in. (63 cm)

American Kestrel
Falco sparverius
To 12 in. (30 cm)

Great Crested Flycatcher
Myiarchus crinitus
To 9 in. (23 cm)

Barn Swallow
Hirundo rustica
To 8 in. (20 cm)
Note deeply
forked tail.

Black-capped Chickadee
Poecile atricapillus
To 6 in. (15 cm)
Name-saying call
is – chick-a-dee-
dee-dee.

Carolina Wren
Thryothorus ludovicianus
To 6 in. (15 cm)
Note white eyebrow
stripe and wing bars.

House Wren
Troglodytes aedon
To 5 in. (13 cm)

White-breasted Nuthatch
Sitta carolinensis
To 6 in. (15 cm)

Tufted Titmouse
Baeolophus bicolor
To 6 in. (15 cm)

Common Grackle
Quiscalus quiscula
To 14 in. (35 cm)

American Crow
Corvus brachyrhynchos
To 22 in. (55 cm)
Call is a distinct – caw.

Blue Jay
Cyanocitta cristata
To 14 in. (35 cm)

Red-winged Blackbird
Agelaius phoeniceus
To 9 in. (23 cm)

European Starling
Sturnus vulgaris
To 8 in. (20 cm)

Gray Catbird
Dumetella carolinensis
To 9 in. (23 cm)
Note black cap and
reddish undertail feathers.

Northern Mockingbird
Mimus polyglottos
To 11 in. (28 cm)

American Robin
Turdus migratorius
To 11 in. (28 cm)

Eastern Bluebird
Sialia sialis
To 7 in. (18 cm)

Common Yellowthroat
Geothlypis trichas
To 5 in. (13 cm)

Scarlet Tanager
Piranga olivacea
To 7 in. (18 cm)

House Sparrow
Passer domesticus
To 6 in. (15 cm)

Baltimore Oriole
Icterus galbula
To 8 in. (20 cm)

American Goldfinch
Spinus tristis
To 5 in. (13 cm)

Cedar Waxwing
Bombycilla cedrorum
To 7 in. (18 cm)
Red wing marks
look like waxy
droplets.

Eastern Towhee
Pipilo erythrophthalmus
To 9 in. (23 cm)
Cheerful song is –
drink-your-tea or drink-tea.

Rose-breasted Grosbeak
Pheucticus ludovicianus
To 9 in. (23 cm)

House Finch
Haemorhous mexicanus
To 6 in. (15 cm)

Dark-eyed Junco
Junco hyemalis
To 7 in. (18 cm)

Evening Grosbeak
Coccothraustes vespertinus
To 8 in. (20 cm)

Northern Cardinal
Cardinalis cardinalis
To 9 in. (23 cm)

Virginia Opossum
Didelphis virginiana
To 40 in. (1 m)

Big Brown Bat
Eptesicus fuscus
To 5 in. (13 cm)

Tricolored Bat
Perimyotis subflavus
To 3.5 in. (9 cm)

Eastern Chipmunk
Tamias striatus
To 12 in. (30 cm)
Note white stripes
on side and face.

Eastern Gray Squirrel
Sciurus carolinensis
To 20 in. (50 cm)

Fox Squirrel
Sciurus niger
To 28 in. (70 cm)
Note large size and
bushy tail. Largest
squirrel in the U.S.

Eastern Cottontail
Sylvilagus floridanus
To 18 in. (45 cm)

Deer Mouse
Peromyscus maniculatus
To 8 in. (20 cm)
Distinguished by its white
undersides and hairy tail.

House Mouse
Mus musculus
To 8 in. (20 cm)
Introduced pest
has a naked tail.

Woodchuck
Marmota monax To 32 in. (80 cm)

Common Porcupine
Erethizon dorsatum To 3 ft. (90 cm)

Norway Rat
Rattus norvegicus
To 18 in. (45 cm)
Brown to gray
rodent has a
naked tail.

Common Muskrat
Ondatra zibethicus To 2 ft. (60 cm)
Aquatic rodent has a naked, scaly tail.

American Beaver
Castor canadensis To 4 ft. (1.2 m)

Common Raccoon
Procyon lotor To 40 in. (1 m)

Striped Skunk
Mephitis mephitis
To 32 in. (80 cm)

Mink
Neovison vison
To 28 in. (70 cm)
Chin is white.

Long-tailed Weasel
Mustela frenata
To 21 in. (53 cm)
Note brown feet and
yellowish neck.

Northern River Otter
Lontra canadensis
To 52 in. (1.3 m)

Common Gray Fox
Urocyon cinereoargenteus
To 3.5 ft. (1.1 m)
Note black-tipped tail.
**Delaware's state
wildlife animal.**

Red Fox
Vulpes vulpes
To 40 in. (1 m)
Note white-tipped tail.

Coyote
Canis latrans
To 52 in. (1.3 m)

Bobcat
Lynx rufus
To 4 ft. (1.2 m)

White-tailed Deer
Odocoileus virginianus
To 7 ft. (2.1 m)

Bottlenosed Dolphin
Tursiops truncatus
To 12 ft. (3.6 m)

Harbor Seal
Phoca vitulina
To 6 ft. (1.8 m)

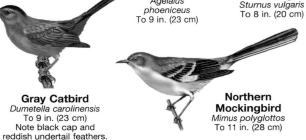

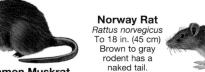

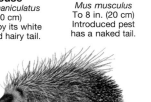